Lighthouse Reflections
A 15 Day Journey of God's Promises

←————————————————————————→

Volume 1 – Lighthouse Reflections Series

Christopher W Corleone

𝔉𝔞𝔩𝔠𝔬𝔫 𝔄𝔯𝔯𝔬𝔴 𝔓𝔲𝔟𝔩𝔦𝔰𝔥𝔦𝔫𝔤

Lighthouse Reflections: A 15 Day Journey of God's Promises
Volume 1 – Lighthouse Reflections Series

Hardback: ISBN-13: 979-8-9859846-2-0
Paperback: ISBN-13: 979-8-9859846-1-3

9 798985 984613

eBook: ISBN-13: 979-8-9859846-0-6

Published in the United States of America.

Publisher: Falcon Arrow Publishing
Editors: Josh Morea
                Shawn Stanaland
Layout: Author
Cover Design: Author

Table of Contents

Forward

Well to be honest, this book originally started out as a prayer journal, but through much prayer and nudging of the Holy Spirit, I felt that God was pulling me in a different direction to help give people a practical, down to earth, back to basic understanding of His promises. Because people nowadays seem to be out of touch with God and it is my hope that this book will help put them back on the righteous path.

This book doesn't assume any experience of reading the Bible. The goal here is not to transmit historical knowledge or textual insight, just basic understanding. It's designed for people reading that are new believers, those who are unsure and thinking about it, those who may have lost their way and even those faithful believers who simply need a refresher on Gods promises.

It is also not a devotional although it can be used as one but seeks to offer a basic understanding of God and some of His promises throughout a 15-day journey. The mission of this book is evangelical. It is meant to introduce a basic unveiling of Gods characteristics throughout each promise and selected scriptural verses, leading all readers to a life-changing encounter with Him.

In this world we live in there is nothing more certain than "death". However, if you lean on God's promises you can be certain of your eternal salvation.

Having a thankful heart can change your entire perspective and outlook on life. One of the best ways to experience the power of thanksgiving is through prayer. Even in the midst of the COVID-19 pandemic - with job loss, sickness and personal loss, we can experience blessings. When we offer a prayer of thanks to God, our focus shifts from our problems to our blessings. And that's the beauty of faith - we can experience gratitude and give thanks despite the circumstances and storms that surround us. (biblestudytools)

We are given many choices and opportunities each and every day to give God thanks. We should be expressing our gratitude daily for His love and faithfulness by helping us overcome the storms and turmoil in our lives. To thank God for the hope and joy regardless of how we may be feeling in the moment. Let Him change your heart and strengthen you with HIS peace and promises.

The best way to defeat Satan's attacks of disappointment, fear and worry is through a grateful heart along with wearing God's armor! We surely have so much to be thankful for because of the gift of salvation through Jesus Christ and the peace He offers. To Him who saves us by grace, we lift-up this prayer: Prayer of Thanks and Gratitude to God

Heavenly Father, thank You for caring about us. Thank You for giving us Your Son that through Him we can have a relationship with You and talk to You about everything. As believers we always have tons of concerns and personal prayers that we bring to You. But all-in-all we are extremely grateful for the promise of peace that you give us. We give our praise to You and love being in Your presence.

Thank You for the sacrifice you made for us on the cross. Thank You for the multitude of promises you gave us to help us to grow in faith. Thank You for the Sabbath so we can rest and recharge our faith and strength in Your presence. In today's busy and corrupt world, it is by Your Love and Grace that we find truth and mercy. Our hearts overflow with gratitude, and may You continue to present opportunities for us to serve the Kingdom of Heaven. In Jesus' Name, we pray, Amen.

Acknowledgements

Every attempt has been made to credit any sources of copyrighted material used in this book. Some resources used come from unknown authors where no credit can be given, other information websites such as Amazing Facts and Got Questions do not post the author, so credit goes to the hosting site. If any such acknowledgement has been inadvertently omitted or miscredited, receipt of such information would be appreciated.

All scripture quotations are taken from the English Standard Version (ESV) unless otherwise indicated.

"All Scripture is breathed out by God and profitable for teaching, for reproof, for correction, and for training in righteousness, that the man of God may be complete, equipped for every good work." (2 Timothy 3:16-17)

Dedication

This book is dedicated to my loving, beautiful, patient and caring wife Maiko Corleone. She has been there with me through good times and bad, inspired me to write my first book and whose loving kindness has sustained me. She has the most loving, caring and generous heart that surpasses many of the so called "die-hard" Christians I have met. She has fortified my love for God so much more than she could ever imagine, because only God could have given me such a wonderful, loving person.

I'm also thankful for my children; Nicole, Michael, Sabrina and Vincent. They are the best inspiration anyone could ever ask for. They helped me to fortify my faith and to learn lessons that only children can teach. They helped me to see God through their eyes, with a faith and innocence that only children possess. They are my heart and I hope that they will remember my words and love long after this mortal shell is but dust and bones.

I dedicate, with reverence, this simple book of God's promises to my family, that without them and the love they shared, this book would still be in the draft and design phase, possibly a distant memory.

Introduction

To help understand the similarity between God's word and a lighthouse; Lighthouses were built to guide men through perilous times in the darkness of this world, just like God's word, a light unto your feet and a lamp unto your path.

"And I will lead the blind in a way that they do not know, in paths that they have not known I will guide them. I will turn the darkness before them into light, the rough places into level ground. These are the things I do, and I do not forsake them." (Isaiah 42:16)

"Wisdom is the right use of knowledge. To know is not to be wise. Many men know a great deal and are all the greater fools for it. There is no fool so great a fool as a knowing fool. But to know how to use knowledge is to have wisdom." - Charles Spurgeon

Embrace - to accept a belief willingly and enthusiastically.

The Bible is full of promises. Some studies show there are approximately, 3,573 and others say up to 7,000. And to put it bluntly, no matter the exact amount, each one of those promises are for believers. And through Christ, every promise has been fulfilled.

"For all the promises of God find their Yes in him. That is why it is through him that we utter our Amen to God for his glory." (2 Corinthians 1:20)

This means all 3,573 or more promises are finished, complete in Christ. If you are a Christian or a believer, there is no single promise of God given to you to fulfill because no man has what it takes to fulfill God's promises.

Why you ask? Because look at what happened in the garden with Adam and Eve. The devil makes it too easy for humankind to fail. So therefore, it's easy to blame the devil for our inadequacies, and yet probably more true that many promises are left personally unfulfilled because we are ignorant, self-centered, egotistical and neglect to embrace the promises of God even though our lives literally depend on it.

So, Jesus said to the Jews who had believed him, "If you abide in my word, you are truly my disciples, and you will know the truth, and the truth will set you free." (John 8:32)

The following promises are truths you should know, to hold onto and include in your daily thoughts. Of all 3,573 promises, start with these because they will set you free. Embrace them, claim them, and memorize them with enthusiasm.

Keep and hide them in your heart, hold them tightly, refusing to let these promises slip past your life. Because as you believe and embrace these promises from God's Word, you will be set free.

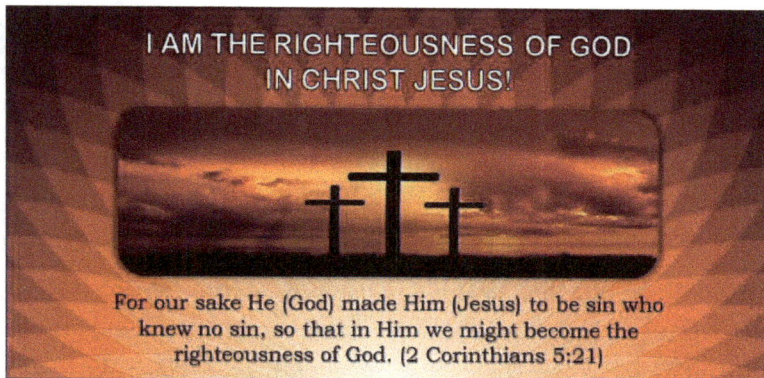

I AM THE RIGHTEOUSNESS OF GOD IN CHRIST JESUS!

For our sake He (God) made Him (Jesus) to be sin who knew no sin, so that in Him we might become the righteousness of God. (2 Corinthians 5:21)

Day 1:

You are the righteousness of God through your belief in Christ.

How exactly is righteousness obtained?

Righteousness is the condition of being in a relationship with the Lord. This can only occur through total faith and dependence upon Christ. To put it mildly simple, we are not made righteous by the things we do. Righteousness is a gift that comes from our Lord, Jesus Christ, to those who accept what He has done for them by faith.

"But now the righteousness of God has been manifested apart from the law, although the Law and the Prophets bear witness to it—the righteousness of God through faith in Jesus Christ for all who believe. For there is no distinction: for all have sinned and fall short of the glory of God, and are justified by his grace as a gift, through the redemption that is in Christ Jesus, whom God put forward as a propitiation by his blood, to be received by faith. This was to show God's righteousness, because in his divine forbearance he had passed over former sins." (Romans 3:21-25)

What does it mean to be the righteousness of God in Christ Jesus? It simply means that when God looks at us, He sees us through the eyes of Christ and His finished work of the cross. We are completely accepted by God and are covered with Jesus' righteousness.

A person who is adopted spiritually by the Father, accepts Jesus as his Lord and Savior and is filled with and sealed by the Holy Spirit until the day of redemption. The righteousness of God, in Christ, means that you are justified, declared righteous because you have had your sins cleansed by the blood of Jesus.

"But thanks be to God, that you who were once slaves of sin have become obedient from the heart to the standard of teaching to which you were committed, and, having been set free from sin, have become slaves of righteousness." (Romans 5:17-18)

What can be expected from God when we choose to believe and accept His son, Jesus? The Word says, "WE ARE" the righteousness of God through our belief in Christ."

"For our sake he made him to be sin who knew no sin, so that in him we might become the righteousness of God." (2 Corinthians 5:21)

What this means is that anyone who believes in Christ has been reconciled and put in righteous standing with God not based on their own works (what they do or don't do) but based on what Christ has done which is the only form of righteousness acceptable to God (aka: The Righteousness of God).

This promise wants you to fully embrace your righteousness through faith in Christ. That you are not a sinner, but God's righteousness through the blood of Jesus. All sins, past, present, and future are covered and forgiven by the blood. No matter what you've done, you are righteous today if you believe in Christ. But the fact is, do we really believe this?

Or is there still a little voice that tries to get us to believe we need to add a tad bit of "works" to close the deal on our righteousness? For those just in case moments when you feel conflicted and knowing you cannot improve upon the finished work of Christ with your works, instead, pray on the promise of righteousness gifted to you by God through Christ and recharge your faith.

Finally, why as a believer, is it important to be righteous?

Because through the power of the Holy Spirit, righteousness allows us to share in the character of Christ, to act in accordance with divine law and morality. The righteousness of Christ does more than just save us; it helps us become the person God intends for us to be.

Daily Meditation and Reflection:

Why am I righteous because of my belief in Christ? How do my righteous actions affect those around me?

YOU ARE A NEW CREATION

Therefore, if anyone is in Christ, he is a new creation. The old has passed away; behold, the new has come.
(2 Corinthians 5:17)

Day 2:

You are a New Creation in Christ.

To be "In Christ," has a great amount of meaning in it. One might ask, "How do I come to be 'in Christ?'" It can be said that our relationship to Christ is molded by our faith, as such, when someone gives themselves totally to Christ (whether they sink or swim), giving their soul completely to the care of the LORD, when they depend on Christ and on Christ alone, not on their works or traditions, but on Christ Jesus; then such a person is in Christ.

We might be in Christ like a brick is to a building. The brick is built into the wall and the wall becomes part of the foundation. The brick and mortar, become part of a wall, a building, that is built on a foundation. That is what it is to be in Christ: it is to trust him for our eternal salvation, just as Noah trusted the ark. To be United with Him as the brick leans on the foundation, becoming an indispensable part of the entire building (body of Christ). To be in Christ is to obtain life from Him as the leaf does from the branch.

"Therefore, if anyone is in Christ, he is a new creation. The old has passed away; behold, the new has come. All this is from God, who through Christ reconciled us to himself and gave us the ministry of reconciliation; that is, in Christ God was reconciling the world to himself, not counting their trespasses against them, and entrusting to us the message of reconciliation." (2 Corinthians 5:17-19)

As the righteousness of God through belief in Christ, you are a new creation. You were a sinner, full of sinful desires, but that was the old you. Now through belief, you are righteous and desire righteousness. You were weak but now you are strong. Your life is changed, a new chapter has begun. As new creations in Christ we are called to put on our new self because we are created to be like God. We become more like God by implementing the teachings of Jesus into our life.

"What shall we say then? Are we to continue in sin that grace may abound? By no means! How can we who died to sin still live in it? Do you not know that all of us who have been baptized into Christ Jesus were baptized into his death? We were buried therefore with him by baptism into death, in order that, just as Christ was raised from the dead by the glory of the Father, we too might walk in newness of life." (Romans 6:4)

Paul tells us that all believers have died with Christ and no longer live for themselves. Our lives are no longer worldly; but now we are spiritual. Our "death" is that of the old sin nature which was nailed to the cross with Christ. It was buried with Him, and just as He was raised up by the Father, so are we raised up to "walk in newness of life".

What does it mean to be a new creation? A "new creation" in Christ means that you now become a cherished son or daughter of God. This means you are no longer dominated by your sinful nature but are now controlled by the Holy Spirit because you have the Spirit of the Living God dwelling on the inside of you. Pray always as if you are a new believer each day to refuel and renew your faith and strength as a new creation.

How is this "new creation" accomplished? It is through the believer in Christ, finding themselves completely pardoned of their past, present, and future sin as a result of their faith in the precious blood of Jesus, loves Christ and the God who gave Christ to be his redemption, which allows that love to become a master passion.

We all have heard of the explosive power and new affection of love for God coming into the soul, expels sin and replaces it with love. It enters the heart of man with such a majestic elegance surrounding it that it puts away man's weakness towards evil, as well as his preconceptions about God, and with a real divine power, it reigns within the soul.

Daily Meditation and Reflection:

What evidence is there in my life that proves that I am a New Creation in Christ?

GOD'S PROMISE OF PROTECTION

The Lord is my rock and my fortress and my deliverer, my God, my rock, in whom I take refuge, my shield, and the horn of my salvation, my stronghold. (Psalm 18:2)

Day 3:

The Promise of Protection.

Have you ever felt like you were left alone and all those friends who said they would stand by you no matter what were nowhere to be found when you needed them the most? Well don't misplace your faith in the same manner, the Lord will always be there to guide you, to keep you on the righteous path and be our protector.

"But the Lord is faithful. He will establish you and guard you against the evil one." (2 Thessalonians 3:3)

God promises protection. In an uncertain world, you have the certainty of God's protection. As Christ-followers, we serve a God who is not surprised by the things we face each day. God is omniscient (all-knowing), so he knows all about every panic, trap, temptation, deadly disease, chaos, confusion, that may threaten your life. Yet He is with us no matter what we face.

"The Lord is my rock and my fortress and my deliverer, my God, my rock, in whom I take refuge, my shield, and the horn of my salvation, my stronghold." (Psalm 18:2)

We can place our trust in Him and find refuge from the storms of this worldly life. This tells us that if God is our refuge and we're kept safely in the arms of His divine protection, then nothing can get through to us unless it goes through God first.

"Fear not, for I am with you; be not dismayed, for I am your God; I will strengthen you, I will help you, I will uphold you with my righteous right hand." (Isaiah 41:10)

With so many promises that God will keep us safe, protect us, and never leave us, it's no surprise that His people have many stories of His protection at work in their lives. But no matter how careful you are or how well you maintain yourself, you will encounter trials. More-often-than-not, we can't see the dangers right in front of us in terms of what will happen in the next one or two minutes in life.

But God who is All-knowing, All-wise and All-powerful, knows and sees all things. He makes it possible for us to avoid those situations that lead us into danger or trouble by either redirecting our path or even preventing us from moving at all.

"The Lord will rescue me from every evil deed and bring me safely into his heavenly kingdom. To him be the glory forever and ever. Amen." (2 Timothy 4:18)

God gave us His Written Living Word, so we can refer to it any time we need reassurance of His presence. Through His word we find promises that proclaim who He is and how He helps us in all circumstances. It is a good feeling to know in times of trouble, when we feel shaky with life's circumstances, that God is our rock, our fortress, and our protector. Seek out His protection through prayer when you feel afflicted and even when you don't as part of your daily walk.

Daily Meditation and Reflection:

How do we receive and apply God's protection, or do we have it naturally as a Child of God when we become a Christian? How do I live under the protection of God?

(This page was intentionally left blank for note taking)

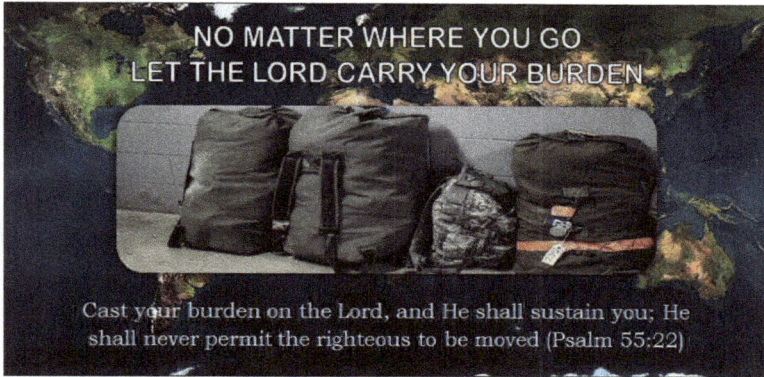

NO MATTER WHERE YOU GO
LET THE LORD CARRY YOUR BURDEN

Cast your burden on the Lord, and He shall sustain you; He shall never permit the righteous to be moved (Psalm 55:22)

Day 4:

Lessen our burdens, let the Lord carry them for you.

What do you do when things get too overwhelming during the day? We're instructed to help each other. Jesus calls us to share each other's burdens. But what does that really mean? It means that as humans we are prone to suffering of one sort or another. Jesus says to bear one another's burdens.

"Bear one another's burdens, and so fulfill the law of Christ. For if anyone thinks he is something, when he is nothing, he deceives himself." (Galatians 6:2-3)

Does that mean He calls us to solve everyone else's problems? No, however, it does mean to be aware and empathetic to others needs over your own. It doesn't mean to allow others to take advantage of you. It means to try to be someone who actually listens with empathy because it can be very therapeutic for someone who is suffering.

You cannot solve everyone's problems, but you can lend your ear and be a voice of reason when others can't make heads or tails out of a situation. With an open heart and your mind engaged, the right words will come as you show you're listening, and you care.

When you help others, you might begin to feel overwhelmed with your own life. But Jesus says to lay it on him and let him carry your burdens. Jesus said we can cast all of our cares on him because he cares for us!

"Cast your burden on the Lord, and He shall sustain you; He shall never permit the righteous to be moved" (Psalm 55:22)

The story of how God organizes help in the desert with Moses is a good example about lessening our burdens. God was well aware of the burden Moses carried as he led the Israelites out of Egypt, so He gathered people to help. God says to Moses "And I will come down and talk with you there. And I will take some of the Spirit that is on you and put it on them, and they shall bear the burden of the people with you, so that you may not bear it yourself alone."

Moses was not meant to carry his burden alone, so God surrounded him with people to help!

"Is this not the fast that I have chosen: To loose the bonds of wickedness, to undo the heavy burdens, to let the oppressed go free, and that you break every yoke?" (Isaiah 58:6)

God is only too happy to carry your burdens and give you the daily strength you need. Life is tough, and the burdens that ensue can sometimes be extremely hard to bear. But you don't have to carry them alone. It must be understood that it's not God's will that we should be crushed down with excessive burdens; let Him free you today. Jesus will remove your heavy burden of guilt and hopelessness and give you true rest in Him.

"Come to Me, all you who labor and are heavy laden, and I will give you rest. Take My yoke upon you and learn from Me, for I am gentle and lowly in heart, and you will find rest for your souls. For My yoke is easy and My burden is light" (Matthew 11:28–30)

God promises to support and help you through every trial. Just knowing your heavenly Father cares about you personally can make any load seem lighter. The Lord desires to constantly support us throughout our lives with the intention of saving us eternally. That's what God is offering you, a chance to lift your burdens, so your walk on the righteous path will be a little smoother.

Remember, when you pray for your burdens to be lightened, God will put others in your path to help you so your daily walk with Christ is uninterrupted.

Daily Meditation and Reflection:

What benefit do I get by letting the Lord carry/handle my burdens?

BREAK FREE
NO MORE CONDEMNATION

There is therefore now no condemnation for those who are in Christ Jesus. For the law of the Spirit of life has set you free in Christ Jesus from the law of sin and death. (Romans 8:1-2)

Day 5:

No More Condemnation.

How do you explain the meaning of "No More Condemnation" to help someone or others understand what God is promising us? Well for starters it's an assurance for those who put their continued faith and belief in Christ that we won't be separated from the love of God.

Since Christ is free from condemnation (sinless) before God, so is the sinner who is "in Christ". Meaning that once we believe and put our faith and trust in Christ, our sins, no matter how small, are forgiven and we are no longer punished (condemned) for our sin. On top of that, Paul tells us,

"But God, being rich in mercy, because of the great love with which he loved us, even when we were dead in our trespasses, made us alive together with Christ—by grace you have been saved— and raised us up with him and seated us with him in the heavenly places in Christ Jesus," (Ephesians 2:4-6)

Being in Christ by faith removes God's condemnation for our sins (trespasses) and assures us of eternal life in heaven. As an example, in Romans 8:35, Paul asks the question, "Who shall separate us from the love of Christ?" He summarizes his answer in verses 38-39, "For I am sure that neither death nor life, nor angels nor rulers, nor things present nor things to come, nor powers, nor height nor depth, nor anything else in all creation, will be able to separate us from the love of God in Christ Jesus our Lord."

"No More Condemnation" can be defined in legal terminology. To have "No More Condemnation" is a declaration to be found innocent of the accusation (crime), to have no sentence awarded and no guilty verdict found.

By the grace of God, believers in Jesus Christ will not face the condemnation of God. When we place our faith in Jesus Christ, we are freed from all condemnation, and assured of God's love. Paul expresses this fact:

"There is therefore now no condemnation for those who are in Christ Jesus. For the law of the Spirit of life has set you free in Christ Jesus from the law of sin and death." (Romans 8:1-2)

One of the Devil's biggest weapons is condemnation. The devil is the accuser. He is quick to condemn you by bringing up your past mistakes and sin. He is quick to accuse you of not being worthy of eternal salvation. However, there is no condemnation to those who are in Christ. Push back the voice of guilt and condemnation with this promise.

To be "in Christ Jesus" means, for purposes of divine judgment, we do not stand before God alone, but with the righteousness of Christ himself. As believers, we have received a righteousness from God that is by faith. (Romans 1:17) So, in Christ, our sins have been forgiven and there is no condemnation.

Since Christ is free from condemnation before God and so are we, the sinner who is "in Christ Jesus". The Bible teaches that everyone will be brought before the judgment throne of God for an ultimate and decisive judgment but those with faith in Christ are removed from God's condemnation and assured of eternal life in heaven.

Daily Meditation and Reflection:

Are there any moments when you felt condemned by someone?
How about when you condemned someone? Do you listen to the
voice of self-condemnation?

YOU WILL NOT BE TAKEN FROM GOD'S HAND

I give them eternal life, and they will never perish, and no one will snatch them out of my hand. (John 10:28)

Day 6:

You cannot be plucked out of God's Hand.

Jesus makes it quite clear that the eternal life He offers is permanent. He holds His sheep (believers) in His hand, and no one, not even the devil can pluck (take) them out of His hand.

All believers (sheep) were given to Jesus by the Father, who is greater than all and who also holds everything created in His hand. Believers are eternally secure, held by the power of God.

"I give them eternal life, and they will never perish, and no one will snatch them out of my hand. My Father, who has given them to me, is greater than all, and no one is able to snatch them out of the Father's hand. I and the Father are one." (John 10:28-30)

Do you ever feel unloved? Unworthy? Our Heavenly Father doesn't see you that way. Nothing can ever separate you from the love of God. No feelings, thoughts, attitude, sinful desires, or any mistake can separate you from the love of God. You cannot escape His love.

It is because of God's great love that He has freely extended the invitation to all people to accept His Son, to believe that Jesus is the savior, the Lord of lords, King of kings and that God raised him from the dead.

By accepting this truth, one becomes saved by grace through faith and receives eternal life. Once you receive eternal life, nothing can change it! No one is going to pluck you out of Christ's hand or out of his Father's hand, not even the devil can steal you away.

To summarize, the faithful believer's eternal salvation was purchased by Christ, secured by the promise of the Father and bonded by the Holy Spirit. The believer's salvation is given and maintained by God's hand, and it's permanent and irrevocable.

The eternal life granted by Jesus, cannot be stolen, revoked, or lost. A believer who places their trust in Jesus Christ as the Savior is declared righteous before God for all eternity and cannot lose his/her salvation.

"For God so loved the world, that he gave his only Son, that whoever believes in him should not perish but have eternal life. For God did not send his Son into the world to condemn the world, but in order that the world might be saved through him." (John 3:16-17)

So when you pray on this promise, always know the Good Shepherd protects His flock, ensuring that no one, not even God's enemies can take them from His hand.

Daily Meditation and Reflection:

What does it mean to not be taken from God's hand? How does it affect your daily living?

(This page was intentionally left blank for note taking)

BLESSED CHILD OF GOD

But to all who did receive him, who believed in his name, he gave the right to become children of God, who were born, not of blood nor of the will of the flesh nor of the will of man, but of God. (John 1:12-13)

Day 7:

You are a Blessed Child of God.

To be called a child of God we simply need to repent of our sins, ask the Lord Jesus Christ to forgive us and then begin to live in faith believing that God has accepted us as His child. The benefits are many as God not only promises to abide with us as we abide in Him but as a child of God, we will also enjoy eternal life.

One of the great parables Jesus spoke about is that of a prodigal son who wasted his inheritance and made an outright a mess of his life. When he returned, he found that not only was his father willing to forgive him, but his father was also willing to restore his wayward child, choosing to love him despite his actions. Our heavenly Father loves each of us in the same way.

"And they were bringing children to him that he might touch them, and the disciples rebuked them. But when Jesus saw it, he was indignant and said to them, "Let the children come to me; do not hinder them, for to such belongs the kingdom of God. Truly, I say to you, whoever does not receive the kingdom of God like a child shall not enter it." And he took them in his arms and blessed them, laying his hands on them." (Mark 10:14-16)

There is no greater teacher than a child if you ever want to learn about child-like faith. Children bless us by the way they indirectly teach us through having childlike faith and a willingness to learn, soaking up information like a sponge. Children are quick to believe because they don't know how not to have faith. They enter this world ready to learn and soak up what we teach them. It's not until they grow older when they naturally start to understand the world.

Having fears, doubts and second guesses comes with unfavorable experiences. So, if you have a child who has lived a good life so far, it's easy for them to believe and be positive because, chances are, that's what they knew at such a young age.

In the same way children are quick to receive, for example, the Kingdom of God, we adults must also be childlike and quick to believe in God's eternal promises. As children of God, we must have full assurance of our salvation.

"But to all who did receive him, who believed in his name, he gave the right to become children of God, who were born, not of blood nor of the will of the flesh nor of the will of man, but of God." (John 1:12-13)

Did you know that we were not always a child of God? Yup, you heard correctly. Of course, He created us, and we are His creatures, but not yet His children! Most of us go through life not really knowing our purpose or even certain we were a true child of God.

One would think that if I was a child of God I should know, right? Not just guess you are or think that you are or maybe you needed to hear someone else call you a child of God before you reacted to (This page was intentionally left blank for note taking)the thought.

Shouldn't we be understanding of this very basic and very important fact? Absolutely, we should be certain, and I hope you consider it too...

Most of us realize who our fathers are on earth, oddly enough because we're all born with earthly fathers. yet in an interesting way, it is the same with God! God created all things, so every person is a creation of God, because He knew each of us before He formed us in our mother's womb.

"For you formed my inward parts; you knitted me together in my mother's womb. I praise you, for I am fearfully and wonderfully made. Wonderful are your works; my soul knows it very well." (Psalm 139:13-14)

"Now the word of the Lord came to me, saying, "Before I formed you in the womb I knew you, and before you were born I consecrated you; I appointed you a prophet to the nations." (Jeremiah 1:14-15)

But just because He knew us before we were formed in the womb, doesn't mean every person is a child of God. All of God's children are born of Him too, but they are born in a spiritual sense! I'm not sure about you, but I wouldn't happy just being a creature of the God of the creation, I would want to be His child. The good news is, we can know for certain that we are a child of God. How do we know? Scripture tells us:

"Everyone who believes that Jesus is the Christ has been born of God, and everyone who loves the Father loves whoever has been born of him. By this we know that we love the children of God, when we love God and obey his commandments." (1 John 5:1-2)

By becoming born again through belief and faith in Christ, we are assured of our place as His children, not just His creation. Pray and meditate on this promise of being a child of God and increase your faith!

Daily Meditation and Reflection:

What makes you a child of God? What changes take place when you become a child of God? How is your attitude towards others after the change?

(This page was intentionally left blank for note taking)

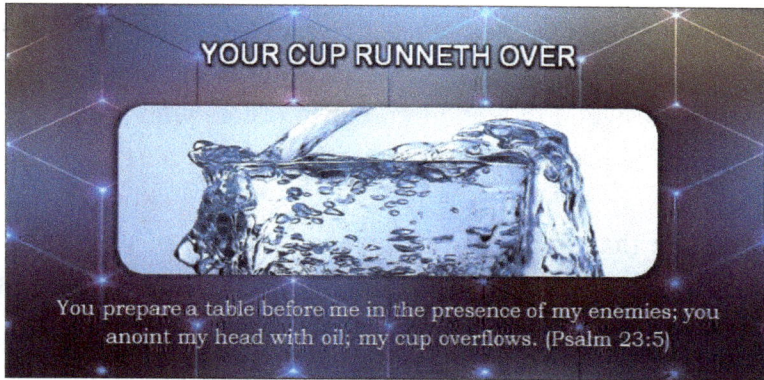

YOUR CUP RUNNETH OVER

You prepare a table before me in the presence of my enemies; you anoint my head with oil; my cup overflows. (Psalm 23:5)

Day 8:

Your Cup Runneth Over.

David describes for us the truth of the wonderful, overflowing blessing He had received from God. Hospitality was highly valued in biblical times with the hosts giving generously from their own food and drink supplies, as seen in Genesis 18.

While psalm uses the image of an overflowing cup of wine, this doesn't necessarily mean that David is talking about material goods.

"You prepare a table before me in the presence of my enemies; you anoint my head with oil; my cup overflows." (Psalm 23:5)

In this instance, David is using this expression to help us understand the abounding and overflowing nature of God's presence, provision, protection and power. God's blessing upon David wasn't just for his life but it was designed to spill over so it could bless others. It is the same with you.

God's blessing is not so that you can hoard it and keep it to yourself. He provides for our needs in abundance, and the overflow of His provision is designed to be poured out to others who are in need. It also is a reminder that God's supply will never run dry.

God has more than enough to help you regardless of your situation. His presence has no boundaries. His provision has no expiration. His protection can't be penetrated. His power has no equal.

Understanding my cup runneth over means you have or are given an abundance (having too much) of something and you can afford to help somebody in need. Which means you have such an abundance of good things or happy benefits that you are overwhelmed by them or cannot contain them.

The message explained in this promise speaks of God's abundant grace and righteous provision in each area of our lives. Showing us that He isn't selfish with His provisions and His blessings are not confined to worldly things. In Christ we can have overflowing joy, overflowing love and overflowing peace.

We can bear everlasting fruit for God's kingdom, and we can overcome impossible challenges when the Holy Spirit fills our hearts until our "cup runneth over." Pray for His continued blessing over your life so you can share with others.

Daily Meditation and Reflection:

What is your understanding of 'your cup runneth over?' What do you do with the excess that God provides?

(This page was intentionally left blank for note taking)

GOD IS ALWAYS WITH US

"Have I not commanded you? Be strong and courageous. Do not be frightened, and do not be dismayed, for the Lord your God is with you wherever you go." (Joshua 1:9)

Day 9:

God is Always with Us.

The divine reality is that God is always with us. However, we don't always recognize His presence in our everyday lives. However, we should be searching for His presence in the tiniest details of our lives, not just when we read His word or worship Him at church.

"Have I not commanded you? Be strong and courageous. Do not be frightened, and do not be dismayed, for the Lord your God is with you wherever you go." (Joshua 1:9)

But is God's presence always with us? God is always present with us. When we put our faith in Jesus, God gives us His Spirit, who dwells with us and in us.

"And I will ask the Father, and he will give you another Helper, to be with you forever, even the Spirit of truth, whom the world cannot receive, because it neither sees him nor knows him. You know him, for he dwells with you and will be in you." (John 14:16-17)

In the stress and the constant "on the go" part of our lives, it can be challenging to recognize God is with us. In short, are we even aware of God's presence in our daily life due to the fast pace we keep? The reality is, God is always with us.

Ultimately, we don't always recognize Him in our everyday lives because our schedules are so full and there is barely enough time to sleep. We sense Him when we read the Bible or go to church, but we overlook His presence in the small details of our daily walks.

Awareness of God's presence can be felt through simple spiritual discipline, by practicing things like Bible study, prayer and especially through praise and worship. It's not mystical or mysterious, and not just for those who spend all their waking hours praying and seeking God, such as monks or nuns.

In fact, being aware of God's presence is for every believer (all who believe, there is no discrimination), because Jesus promised to be with us always. It's known by some as "practicing the presence of God" or simply "communion with God." Scripture reminds us to be in His presence (light).

"Blessed are the people who know the festal shout, who walk, O Lord, in the light of your face, who exult in your name all the day and in your righteousness are exalted. (Psalm 89:15-16)

Rejoice in God's name all day long. But how? This verse gives you a hint: "who walk, O Lord, in the light of your face (presence)". The essential part of "always rejoicing" is by simply acknowledging God's presence throughout the day, praising Him, and thanking Him for being there.

Remember that you don't have to feel ashamed for not being able to pray every second of every day. Just be moved by His kindness and love, pray when you can and be thankful, He is always there through good times and bad.

Daily Meditation and Reflection:

What are some signs that God is always with you? Do you find comfort in knowing He is always there?

DESIGNED FOR A PURPOSE

"For we are his workmanship, created in Christ Jesus for good works, which God prepared beforehand, that we should walk in them." (Ephesians 2:10)

Day 10:

God designed each one of Us for a Purpose.

All Christians are created to serve. We are called, created, saved, and spiritually gifted to fulfill His will.

"For we are his workmanship, created in Christ Jesus for good works, which God prepared beforehand, that we should walk in them." (Ephesians 2:10)

We were created for a purpose for the kingdom: part of our purpose is to worship, serve and make disciples for God's glory.

"Not to us, O Lord, not to us, but to your name give glory, for the sake of your steadfast love and your faithfulness!" (Psalm 115:1)

Through Christ who rose from the dead, offers eternal life to all who have faith and believe in him. Because of our belief and faith, He fills us with the Holy Spirit to help us live out our true identity and purpose in this life.

We have other gifts that God gives us to add depth to our purpose, sadly, many go to their grave never knowing and understanding our purpose.

God created us for a purpose. Our destiny is not simply based on our talents, skills, abilities, gifts, education, wealth or health, though these may be useful. God's plan for our lives is based on God's grace and our response to serve Him. All that we have is a gift from God. What we are is a gift back to him.

"In him we have obtained an inheritance, having been predestined according to the purpose of him who works all things according to the counsel of his will, so that we who were the first to hope in Christ might be to the praise of his glory." (Ephesians 1:11-12)

God's plan is that our lives bring Him glory. He has chosen us, in love, to be a living reflection of Him. Part of our response to Him is our vocation, a particular way of service that allows us to grow in holiness and become more like Him. - Kimberly Hahn

The only way we can begin to become God's master creation is by being born again, where we become a new creation in Christ. Then we can truly start to understand our purpose. The purpose of God saving us and making us new creations in Christ is so that we would produce good works to glorify the Kingdom of Heaven.

Daily Meditation and Reflection:

How would you define your purpose in God's Kingdom?

(This page was intentionally left blank for note taking)

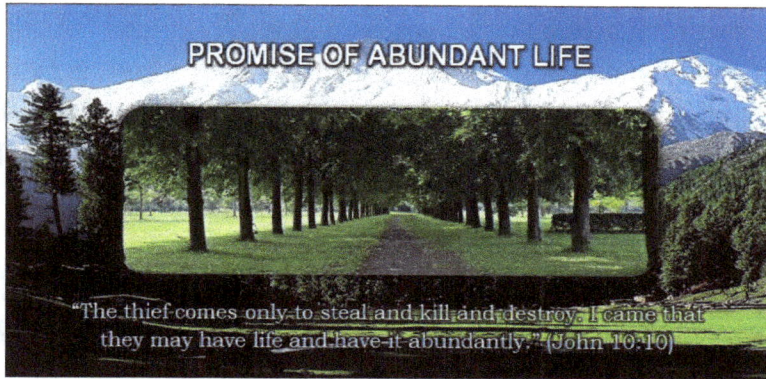

PROMISE OF ABUNDANT LIFE

"The thief comes only to steal and kill and destroy. I came that they may have life and have it abundantly." (John 10:10)

Day 11:

God promises you an Abundant Life.

Unlike a thief, who comes for selfish reasons, Lord Jesus comes to give, not to take. He comes that believers may have life in Him that is meaningful, purposeful, joyful, and eternal. We receive this abundant life the moment we believe and accept Him as our Savior.

"The thief comes only to steal and kill and destroy. I came that they may have life and have it abundantly." (John 10:10)

In the eyes of the believer, Jesus is the source of abundant life. He is our life, our joy and is the reason for eternal hope. He came to give life in fullness, abundance, and prosperity, not just a normal average existence that most people come to expect. To add a little depth, the word abundant life translates from the Greek word perisson or perissos, which means beyond what is anticipated, exceeding expectation; "more abundant," going past the expected limit. (Strongs concordance)

When you totally commit to God, He will totally commit Himself to you. To intimately know Jesus and experience His love, is to know abundant life. God's new covenant for us through Christ, is abundant life. To begin experiencing abundant life and biblical prosperity is to believe it is God's highest desire for you.

God wants us to overflow with His love, goodness and blessing. He desires us to live an abundant life that overflows to bless others. Learn to be content and don't hoard the blessing God provides. After his conversion, Paul learned to live fully and humbly, and how to be content in every situation with what God granted each day.

"Not that I am speaking of being in need, for I have learned in whatever situation I am to be content. I know how to be brought low, and I know how to abound. In any and every circumstance, I have learned the secret of facing plenty and hunger, abundance and need. I can do all things through him who strengthens me." *(Philippians 4:11-13)*

Paul told Timothy "But godliness with contentment is great gain, for we brought nothing into the world, and we cannot take anything out of the world" (1 Tim. 6:6-7)

As you walk with Jesus, don't grumble along the way, be satisfied in every situation as you trust Him. Thank God for every blessing and be content while you wait in faith for answers to your prayers. Complainers lack faith and rarely see mountains move. - Bob Sawvelle

"It is the Spirit who gives life; the flesh is no help at all. The words that I have spoken to you are spirit and life." (John 6:63)

A life of abundance is one that comes from following the ways taught to us by Christ. It means being compassionate toward one another. It means developing a gentle spirit as you go through your life's journey, as well as giving unconditionally of what God has provided to you. Take time in your day to pray and ask God how you can have an abundant life by sharing what He has given you.

Daily Meditation and Reflection:

What does the promise of abundant life mean to you? Does it mean your life on earth will be easy?

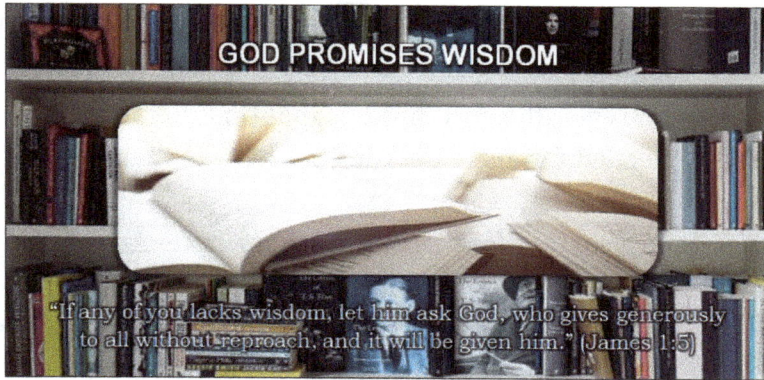

GOD PROMISES WISDOM

"If any of you lacks wisdom, let him ask God, who gives generously to all without reproach, and it will be given him." (James 1:5)

Day 12:

God will give you Wisdom.

If you ever wondered about the wisdom needed to make tough choices, fear not, because the good news is that God promises to give us the wisdom we need for every decision we have to make. So it's a critical point of faith that we pray over God's promises until this fear is conquered, and we can peacefully seek and wait on God for the wisdom he will give.

"If any of you lacks wisdom, let him ask God, who gives generously to all without reproach, and it will be given him. But let him ask in faith, with no doubting, for the one who doubts is like a wave of the sea that is driven and tossed by the wind." (James 1:5-6)

We generally have to make big decisions throughout our lives, some will bring fear, anxiety or cause us to change relationships, such as a career or job-change, deciding which college to attend or maybe it's getting married or having children. Other choices we have are less important but can cause us to miscue, things like friendships, could even be a choice of hobbies, etc.

Because these decisions are huge, sometimes just the fear alone makes us think that we'll make the wrong choice or we won't know what to do. However, the good news is that God promises to give us the wisdom needed for every decision we have to make.

"For the Lord gives wisdom; from his mouth come knowledge and understanding; he stores up sound wisdom for the upright; he is a shield to those who walk in integrity, guarding the paths of justice and watching over the way of his saints." (Proverbs 2:6-8)

Some find it confusing when they hear scripture explaining the "Fear of God is the beginning of knowledge". In other words, why would God want me to be scared of Him? The Hebrew word for fear in these verses is "Yirah". What does Yirah mean? The Hebrew word translated into 'awe' in the Bible is yirah (3374, pronounced yir-ah).

It often directly translates into fear, but it can also mean respect, reverence, and worship. In this context, it is our reverence and respect for God that motivates us to do His will. Knowing the original language changes our perspective of the scripture!

It's extremely important to fight the fight of faith by praying over God's promises until this fear is conquered, and we can peacefully seek and wait on God for the wisdom He will give.

Daily Meditation and Reflection:

How does God's guidance through wisdom make you change the way you think? What are some practical decisions you have made based upon God's wisdom?

(This page was intentionally left blank for note taking)

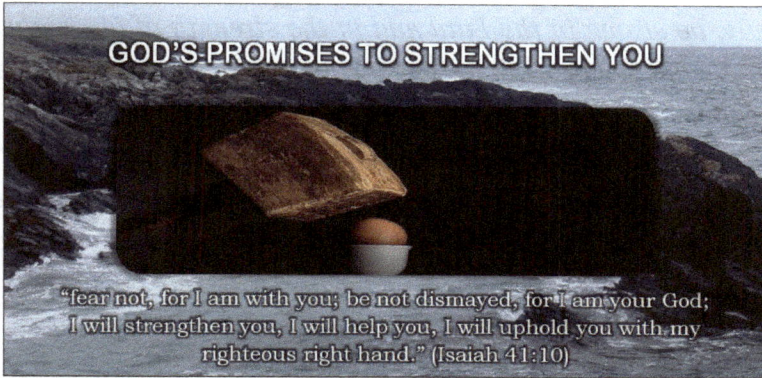

GOD'S PROMISES TO STRENGTHEN YOU

"fear not, for I am with you; be not dismayed, for I am your God;
I will strengthen you, I will help you, I will uphold you with my
righteous right hand." (Isaiah 41:10)

Day13:

God's promise to Strengthen and Help You.

Every new day we're reminded of our weaknesses. Remember that no human has ever lived a perfect day. But the blessing of this promise lies in the fact that God promises his strength when we are weak. Being in His grace allows us to live with the real, meaningful and powerful strength of God.

"fear not, for I am with you; be not dismayed, for I am your God; I will strengthen you, I will help you, I will uphold you with my righteous right hand." (Isaiah 41:10)

You might ask yourself, "How can we be strengthened in the Lord?" We can strengthen ourselves by renewing our mind, led by the Holy Spirit in order to know and understand God's will and destiny for our lives. We can renew our hearts by studying God's word learning compassion for others. When we focus on Him, and what He's done for us in our lives, we can move from strength to strength no matter our circumstances.

"Finally, be strong in the Lord and in the strength of his might. Put on the whole armor of God, that you may be able to stand against the schemes of the devil. For we do not wrestle against flesh and blood, but against the rulers, against the authorities, against the cosmic powers over this present darkness, against the spiritual forces of evil in the heavenly places. Therefore, take up the whole armor of God, that you may be able to withstand in the evil day, and having done all, to stand firm." (Ephesians 6:10-13)

Ephesians 6 tells us we have a formidable adversary in this world, whether you see him or believe in his existence. Therefore, we need to put on the whole Armor of God. Keeping in mind the devil is always on the prowl:

"Be sober-minded; be watchful. Your adversary the devil prowls around like a roaring lion, seeking someone to devour." (1 Peter 5:8)

The devil commands the "spiritual forces of evil" to purposely trip us up, in every effort to separate us from God. But this should not invoke fear because we know how this story ends. Jesus has claimed victory over Death and Satan by way of the cross and will defeat him finally during His return to call His people home. Until then, the spiritual battle continues, and we need to put on God's armor and get in the battle as Defenders.

After all, we must understand that we have advantages in this battle. We are not acting as Defenders with inferior weapons. Our commander Jesus Christ provides everything we need to fight off the devil's assaults: the belt of truth, the breastplate of righteousness, the boots of the gospel of peace, the shield of faith, the helmet of salvation and the sword of the Spirit.

"Therefore, take up the whole armor of God, that you may be able to withstand in the evil day, and having done all, to stand firm. Stand therefore, having fastened on the belt of truth, and having put on the breastplate of righteousness, and, as shoes for your feet, having put on the readiness given by the gospel of peace. In all circumstances take up the shield of faith, with which you can extinguish all the flaming darts of the evil one; and take the helmet of salvation, and the sword of the Spirit, which is the word of God, praying at all times in the Spirit, with all prayer and supplication."
(Ephesians 6:14-18)

Continuous reading and study of God's word along with prayer holds our armor together, providing all the protection we need.

But don't think in terms of simply withstanding the devil's attacks, our armor is not only for defense, it also allows us to take the fight directly to him. Instead of allowing the devil to instill within us a fear that paralyzes with inaction, let the knowledge we know about our enemy spur us into action and take the offensive.

Matter of fact, our sword is one piece of armor that is a dual weapon, which can be used both for defense and offense. It's called, "The Sword of the Spirit", which represents the Word of God! Jesus used this sword when the devil attacked Him three times in the desert with deception, but three times Jesus deflected and counter-attacked, quoting Scripture, declaring God's steadfast truth: He took His stand, used His sword, and defeated Satan.

Are you reading God's Word daily? Can you counter the enemy's attacks by recalling Scripture, which we know is sharper than any two-edged sword? As a Defender you must know Scripture, and how to use it to counter the enemy's attack.

Satan will flee when we resist him by relying on the truths of Scripture and the power of prayer. Instead of being preoccupied with what Satan is doing next, we should be thinking about what we're going to do next. All that is needed is for you to take a stand, draw your sword, and rely on the Lord in this epic battle for souls. Know the Commander of our Faith will be leading the attack on the enemy. As Christ leads the charge, put on your ARMOR and fall in behind Him!

"being strengthened with all power, according to his glorious might, for all endurance and patience with joy; giving thanks to the Father, who has qualified you to share in the inheritance of the saints in light. He has delivered us from the domain of darkness and transferred us to the kingdom of his beloved Son, in whom we have redemption, the forgiveness of sins." (Colossians 1:11-14)

If we take the time to call upon the Lord, we will find that He provides all the tools we will ever need to strengthen us inside and out. And then we will find the strength during turbulent times. We are strengthened through Christ our redeemer and set apart by His forgiveness of our sin, able to stand firmly against the enemy and win the spiritual battle for souls.

Daily Meditation and Reflection:

How do God's presence and promises strengthen you to answer
His call?

(This page was intentionally left blank for note taking)

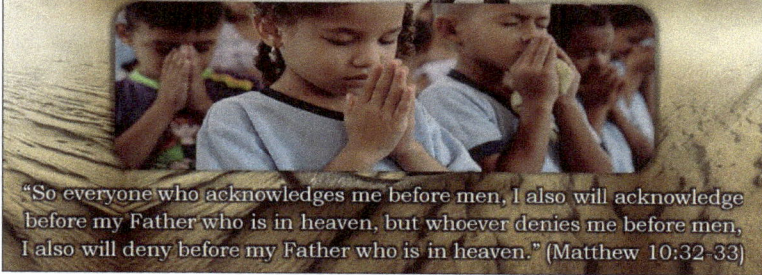

GOD'S PROMISE OF ACKNOWLEDGEMENT AND ACCEPTANCE

"So everyone who acknowledges me before men, I also will acknowledge before my Father who is in heaven, but whoever denies me before men, I also will deny before my Father who is in heaven." (Matthew 10:32-33)

Day 14:

God's promise of Acknowledgement and Acceptance.

For us to be accepted we need to acknowledge Christ first. A big part of acknowledging God in all our ways is to "pray continually". Believe it or not, God loves you. He cares for you and wants a relationship with you so take the time to share with Him your joys, fears, goals, desires, and failures. We can't hide our thoughts from God anyway and we shouldn't try.

"So everyone who acknowledges me before men, I also will acknowledge before my Father who is in heaven, but whoever denies me before men, I also will deny before my Father who is in heaven." (Matthew 10:32-33)

Our world knows brokenness and sin to almost every extent, new ways that enhance the old are constantly changing the way sin looks, but our never changing God offers hope and restoration. A favorite verse spoken by many is:

"For I know the plans I have for you, declares the Lord, plans for welfare and not for evil, to give you a future and a hope." (Jeremiah 29:11)

God says, "For I know the plans I have for you, plans to prosper you and not to harm you, plans to give you hope and a future." God's plan for your life includes hope and a prosperous future or one in which you thrive. But you ask, "What's the catch?" Well, glad you asked. The catch is you must acknowledge that Jesus is Lord. Not just to yourself, because that in itself doesn't necessarily cause change.

But when you proclaim it to others, as Jesus tells us, "everyone who acknowledges me before men, I also will acknowledge before my Father who is in heaven", "but whoever denies me before men, I also will deny before my Father who is in heaven", with that understanding, then change can occur.

Keep in mind that Jesus will say one of two things. Either he will acknowledge you or he will disown you. To acknowledge you means he will accept you as a child of God and say to the Father "This is (insert your name here), and he/she belongs to me." To disown (deny) you means Jesus will say to the Father "This is (insert your name here), and he has nothing to do with me, I never knew him."

Every person will hear the Son of God say one of these two things. Jesus makes it clear what he says about you then is intimately tied to what you say about him now: "Whoever acknowledges me before men (what we say about Jesus now), I will also acknowledge him before my Father in heaven (what Jesus will say about you then).

Psalm 103 lists many ways that God wants to bless you. Psalm 103 exclaims, "Bless the Lord, O my soul, and all that is within me, bless his holy name! Bless the Lord, O my soul, and forget not all his benefits, who forgives all your iniquity, who heals all your diseases, who redeems your life from the pit, who crowns you with steadfast love and mercy, who satisfies you with good so that your youth is renewed like the eagle's."

God is invested in your well-being and working toward your renewal, wholeness and healing daily. In addition to blessing us, God has big plans for our lives and calls us to follow. Obedience often requires faith and risk, but God will delight in your dependence on Him and will always be there to support you. The only requirement is that we accept His son Jesus and give acknowledgement to others that He is our Savior.

Jesus tells us, "I am the way, and the truth, and the life. No one comes to the Father except through me." (John 14:6), you say "For me, Jesus is my way and my truth and my life." You must believe it. You must own it. You don't say "This is what Jesus says but I have a different view" or "I'm not sure about that." Because we know through our belief and acknowledgement, He will stand with us during final judgment, that's His promise to us the faithful.

We live in a culture of uncertainty, and much doubt. Yet it is comfortable for us to be self-reliant, not depending on others. But if you want Christ to confess and acknowledge (accept) you in heaven, then at some point you have to move from being self-reliant to being a confessor: In other words, Jesus puts it like this, "If you acknowledge me, then I will accept you..." not "if you consider me..."

"But the one who did not know, and did what deserved a beating, will receive a light beating. Everyone to whom much was given, of him much will be required, and from him to whom they entrusted much, they will demand the more." (Luke 12:48)

But it's not just confessing Jesus is Lord, because that's easy. Talk is cheap. Jesus never said following Him would be easy, it will require much work. In addition, you must acknowledge Him before men, in order for Him to acknowledge you to the Father in heaven. So, as you pray on this promise, be prepared to pick up your cross and follow Him.

Daily Meditation and Reflection:

What is the significance of acknowledging God before all decisions? Why is it important that we acknowledge God before He acknowledges us?

(This page was intentionally left blank for note taking)

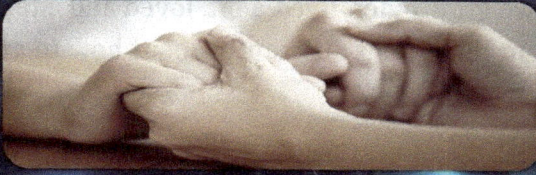

GOD'S PROMISE OF
KINDNESS, COMPASSION, AND MERCY

"The Lord is merciful and gracious, slow to anger and abounding in steadfast love." (Psalm 103:8)

Day 15:

God promises Kindness, Compassion, and Mercy.

How does someone explain compassion from the Lord? Compassion is kindness and sympathy, but it goes deeper, more powerful in its meaning. The origin of compassion helps us understand the true importance.

The Latin root for the word compassion is pati, which means to suffer, and the prefix com- means with. Compassion, originating from compati, literally means to suffer with. Compassion means someone else's heartbreak becomes your heartbreak. Another's suffering becomes your suffering. True compassion changes the way we live.

"The Lord is merciful and gracious, slow to anger and abounding in steadfast love." (Psalm 103:8)

To understand God's promise of kindness, compassion and mercy, we look to the one who sacrificed everything showing us how to live according to Gods will. Remember that Jesus was the one who suffered and died on a cross for us.

What can we do, or better yet, how can we express our devotion and love to Him in a way that would show our resolve, dedication, and love? As we grow older, lived a bit, loved and experienced hurt, we've learned to think a bit differently about how to approach truth and lies.

We see things all around that help us grasp the harsh reality that is sometimes expressed many different ways in our world. However, there is also a gentleness and tenderness that we can find if we simply open our eyes. So, what if we approached this understanding with a desire to be gentle to ourselves, to assess our failings with kindness and tenderly correct ourselves? In other words, look at everything through the eyes of Jesus.

"For the mountains may depart and the hills be removed, but my steadfast love shall not depart from you, and my covenant of peace shall not be removed," says the Lord, who has compassion on you." (Isaiah 54:10)

We read and acknowledge through scripture, a God who exhibits clemency (mercy, compassion). Take the parable of the prodigal on, the message of The Prodigal Son is that it doesn't matter how far we stray from our Heavenly Father or how much we squander the gifts He provides, He is always delighted when we turn back to Him. His unconditional love and compassion is waiting for us to return home where He greets us with open arms.

But could this be explored from another angle? What if we use this story to discover what a good relationship looks like? What if we examine each of the emotions or feelings that prevent us from seeking reconciliation with others, with ourselves, and most significantly, with our loving God? How would this encourage us to think differently about our own compassion and mercy? Would it make us kinder and more righteous, godlier?

"Praise the Lord, all nations! Extol him, all peoples! For great is his steadfast love toward us, and the faithfulness of the Lord endures forever. Praise the Lord!" (Psalm 117)

Even though this psalm is extremely short, it is rich with truth and wisdom. Psalm 117 speaks to all people with the exhortation (encouragement) to praise the Lord. We are given two reasons for praising God: His merciful kindness toward us and His abiding truth. Think about the meaning of the Lord's merciful kindness.

This phrase, merciful kindness, occurs hundreds of times in the Hebrew scriptures, mostly in Psalms. The term is usually translated as mercy, lovingkindness, or goodness, and in meaning, it covers the New Testament concept of mercy and grace.

We can think of mercy as the withholding of a deserved punishment, or an act of pity towards someone who is disadvantaged, afflicted, or suffering in some way through no fault of their own. Then the biblical concept of grace involves kindness and the free giving of benefits or help that is not necessarily earned, but freely given.

Sometimes unpleasant circumstances, such as we're currently experiencing, especially with the COVID pandemic, can skew our thinking and take away our attention from God's goodness. We are hit daily with bad news and various statistics (people dying, vehicle accidents, etc.). From one day to the next, things can seem to be getting worse, not better.

At such times, we might need to consciously remind ourselves of the mercy the Lord has shown us and the kindnesses He has already bestowed upon us, through Christ. In our prayers upon Gods promises, we should always be thankful we are able receive His kindness, compassion, and mercy throughout each day that we live!

Keeping in mind that Christ didn't have to do any of that. But He did it all for you and I personally, for everyone. It's all mercy and grace: our praise and thanks to Him should flow freely in light of that. He through grace, gave us His righteousness, so that we can say, "I am the righteousness of God through my belief in Christ".

Daily Meditation and Reflection:

How does God show us His mercy and compassion? Do you treat others with the same mercy and compassion as what God has shown you?

(This page was intentionally left blank for note taking)

Thank you and Reviews

A special thank you goes out to the following friends, family and others for their help during the process in the creation of this book. Josh Morea, Shawn Stanaland, Scott Howell, and Stephen Fields

---

"Do all things without grumbling or disputing, that you may be blameless and innocent, children of God without blemish in the midst of a crooked and twisted generation, among whom you shine as lights in the world..." (Philippians 2:14-15)

I have had the privilege of watching the evolution of this book as my brother and his family have faced down circumstances that would have easily destroyed most modern families. They rise to each new challenge with a sense of humor and grace that is both humbling and inspiring to witness. This book, which I hope is the first of many, is the first foray Chris has taken to convey the passages that bring him strength and have enabled him to not just survive but thrive, leaning on God's promises with strength that is renewed each and every day. – *Shawn Stanaland*

I think my favorite part of this entire work is how anyone can find their place and comfort in what you have put together.

You ask for our favorite part of this writing, and I would have to say, Day 2 and 5. Only because in the ministry God has called me to, that being reaching the "others" in our community. Becoming a "New Creation" is so foreign to many today. They have lived/survived so many catastrophic events in their lives, that they begin to believe there is nothing different, or better. Day 5 is just as impactful to me, because the thought of truly "Breaking Free" seems impossible, and it is in our own strength and abilities. I battled with alcohol, Nicotine (which isn't too taboo any longer), filthy language (see Nicotine).

All these addictions would totally change my behavior, when the "urge" would hit me. Sin will do this to us, and when we get so deep in sin, we cannot see a way out. You are 10 feet under in sin, and hear a preacher tell you "Just surrender it all to Jesus", you have NOTHING to base that on! It is desperately important to have resources like this daily "Journey of God's Promises" for someone who is struggling to find Hope. My struggle is not your struggle, and day 2 and 5 may not speak to you the way it speaks to me. That is one of the great gifts of this book. You can find your comfort somewhere among the pages of this book and allow God to start a healing and restoring process in your life. Read it EVERYDAY. Something will speak new and fresh to you tomorrow. What a gift, Christopher! Be blessed. - *Scott Howell*

Review: Lighthouse Reflections, A 15 Day Journey of God's Promises

In his short devotional journal, Christopher Corleone unpacks fifteen of God's precious promises to His children. Corleone lifts each one of the daily promises directly from the pages of Scripture. Corleone asks poignant, thought-provoking questions, weaves Biblical truths into each day's devotional thought, and follows up with space for the reader's response. Corleone desires for each of his readers to grow closer in his or her walk with the Lord through this fifteen-day journey.

Knowing Christopher Corleone and his family personally through my church, I have tremendous respect for what he has accomplished in this book. Corleone does not simply write about God's promises, but he has built his life upon them. He has overcome enormous obstacles to produce this work. I am proud to call him my friend.

You will be enlightened, encouraged, and inspired on your journey with Christ as you read this book. - *William Joshua Morea, D. Min*

AUTHOR'S NOTE

The idea and principle of the study of God's promises is to reinforce the basic understanding of His character and His righteousness. I encourage everyone to pick up a Bible and read for themselves to learn more about God, Jesus, and the Holy Spirit. I chose the English Standard Version (ESV), but there are other recommended versions such as the KJV and the NKJV.

Reading the Bible on a regular and consistent basis will provide you with several benefits. First, the Bible shows us God's character and provides us God's revelation of Himself to His people. In each section of the Bible, we see God's holy, unchanging, faithful, gracious, and loving character. Studying is helpful because what you read and write down will impact you in wonderous ways.

Secondly, 2 Timothy 3:16-17 when discussing the topic of Scripture says that it is "profitable for teaching, for reproof, for correction and for training in righteousness." The next verse goes on to say that this leads to completeness and equipping "for every good work" (ESV).

Third, regularly reading God's word reorients our thinking so that we can grow in maturity, which is part of the Christian calling (Ephesians 4:14-16; Romans 12:1-2). Have you ever met a mature Christian who did not regularly read the Bible? These three things are just the beginning, this list could include dozens of reasons why you should read the Bible on a regular basis. Such as:

- Cultural literacy
- To learn what it says first-hand
- Personal edification

- To learn about helping others
- Jesus and His purpose
- Because it is God's Word to us
- To know God better
- Avoiding error

Believe me when I say there are plenty of reasons to read and study the Bible, understanding the reason for salvation is a good starting point (Acts 4:12). While not a complete list, these are just a few reasons why reading and studying the Bible is not wasted time.

The question remains, "Why should I read and study the Bible?" Because it is both practical and foundational. As harsh as this may sound, the fact is that one of the greatest threats to a strong and healthy relationship with the Lord is false teaching. False teaching has made its way into the church on the back of the truth by twisting and even outright denying God's Word.

Therefore, its practical because we will understand why reading the Bible is important, but it's also foundational because it will prepare us for future discussions on the importance of Bible study. By continuous reading God will ensure we are better equipped especially when our faith is questioned and tested.

Too many people rely on the scholars and educated ministers (taught in secular Institutions) to give us a better understanding of God's word. But how do you know what they say falls in line with Scripture? The obvious answer is "you don't," unless you read and study the Bible.

God's word is a living word and can be individually interpreted by each reader. However, there is a basic foundation that everyone should know, but in order to get that you must read a little each day. You don't have to attend school to learn Biblical theology. All it takes is 5 minutes a day to start your journey.

A great place to start is to begin by setting aside a regular time to study God's word with a good Bible study tool. There are many free tools that can help you such as phone and pc apps, websites such as biblestudytools.com, biblegateway.com, bible concordances, etc. that can be helpful on your journey. Hopefully this book helps to get you started in the right direction.

Remember to pray and seek God's wisdom before you start. Sometimes the best place to start is during fellowship with other believers and of course your local pastor and his ministry team. My friend, I pray that your journey leads you to salvation and eternal life.

May God bless you in all your endeavors.

Closing Thoughts

It is a great privilege to be able to share God's love through His promises with you over the last fifteen days. I want to thank you for taking time out of your busy schedule each day to receive His words. I hope the powerful truths shared throughout the pages of this book have inspired and encouraged you to seek the love and grace of our Lord Jesus Christ. My friend, remember that searching and understanding God's promises is not about your self-efforts, but all about receiving God's abundant grace and the gift of righteousness through Jesus.

"For if, because of one man's trespass, death reigned through that one man, much more will those who receive the abundance of grace and the free gift of righteousness reign in life through the one-man Jesus Christ." (Romans 5:17)

God has called you to rest in His finished work and overcome every fear, guilt, and or addiction. Whatever challenges you may still be facing, I want to encourage you to keep embracing Christ and His grace toward you. Keep reading about His compassion, love, and finished work on the cross. Keep reading about His awesome promises and plans for you. As the apostle Paul tells us,

"So faith comes from hearing, and hearing through the word of Christ." (Romans 10:17)

My friend, I'll stand beside you in faith. I believe that as you keep receiving God's precious gifts of abundant grace, righteousness, and no condemnation even in the midst of failures, you will experience the fulfillment of His plan for you. And when you do, please write to me (cw.corleone@hotmail.com) so that I can rejoice with you.

I pray the promises shown to you in this book have touched and encouraged your heart, so you can be a source of encouragement to many others who are seeking God. Thank you once again for taking this fifteen-day journey with me. Until next time, my love and prayers are with you and your family.

Yours in Christ,

Christopher W Corleone

www.ingramcontent.com/pod-product-compliance
Lightning Source LLC
Chambersburg PA
CBHW060514280326
41933CB00014B/2959